T0353693

THE
ARTIST'S
BOOK
OF
Wisdom

JIM GARDNER

BALBOA.PRESS
A DIVISION OF HAY HOUSE

Copyright © 2024 Jim Gardner.

All rights reserved. No part of this book may be used or reproduced by any means, graphic, electronic, or mechanical, including photocopying, recording, taping or by any information storage retrieval system without the written permission of the author except in the case of brief quotations embodied in critical articles and reviews.

Balboa Press books may be ordered through booksellers or by contacting:

Balboa Press
A Division of Hay House
1663 Liberty Drive
Bloomington, IN 47403
www.balboapress.com
844-682-1282

Because of the dynamic nature of the Internet, any web addresses or links contained in this book may have changed since publication and may no longer be valid. The views expressed in this work are solely those of the author and do not necessarily reflect the views of the publisher, and the publisher hereby disclaims any responsibility for them.

The author of this book does not dispense medical advice or prescribe the use of any technique as a form of treatment for physical, emotional, or medical problems without the advice of a physician, either directly or indirectly. The intent of the author is only to offer information of a general nature to help you in your quest for emotional and spiritual well-being. In the event you use any of the information in this book for yourself, which is your constitutional right, the author and the publisher assume no responsibility for your actions.

Any people depicted in stock imagery provided by Getty Images are models, and such images are being used for illustrative purposes only.
Certain stock imagery © Getty Images.

Print information available on the last page.

ISBN: 979-8-7652-5205-5 (sc)
ISBN: 979-8-7652-5206-2 (hc)
ISBN: 979-8-7652-5204-8 (e)

Library of Congress Control Number: 2024919519

Balboa Press rev. date: 10/27/2024

Contents

PART 2: GENERAL OBSERVATIONS

PART 3: THE SPIRITUAL SIDE OF THINGS

Introduction

Our talents are our greatest assets, and learning to market them can be our greatest achievement. We all have gifts that we can develop, and by sharing our unique gifts with the world, we can discover the unlimited creative resources within us while we make a positive contribution to the community we live in.

Through the process of developing our talents into something of value to others, we learn more about ourselves, and we discover and develop more of our hidden potential. We continually grow into something greater than we were the day before.

This book is a collection of thoughts that have proven to be helpful for me on my journey and it gives me great pleasure to share them with you here.

It is my hope that they encourage you when you are tired or frustrated and that they will serve to shorten your journey from wherever you are now to wherever you want your talent to take you.

It's the journey as well as the destination that make each day fun and interesting. While the writings in this book are directed toward artistic expression, the lessons in this guidebook are designed to help you chart the direction of your life for whatever work you choose to do.

PART 1

The Business of Art

PART I

Your Talent Is Your Greatest Asset

Your talent is your greatest asset, and learning how to market it can be your greatest achievement! The key to earning money lies in providing a product or a service that other people value. That's true whether you are earning a living as an hourly wage earner who is providing a service to your employer, or if you are an independent vendor, providing a specific product or service directly to the client.

If you look at what you are currently being paid, you will have a good idea of what your service is being valued at. If you want to increase your income, you must find ways to increase the value of your service. We get paid in proportion to the value people place on the products and services we offer. If it is important to them, they will be willing to pay a higher price for it. If it has little value to them, they will only pay a small price or not be willing to buy it at all.

So, if we want to earn money, the question we must ask ourselves is, "How can I make my talent more valuable to others?" We all want to earn money, and we are all here to serve others in some way. As creative people, we have been blessed with our own unique gifts and our own unique lessons to learn.

If we use our gifts, we will learn our lessons, and life will be full of interesting and rewarding experiences. We will discover deeper parts of ourselves as we develop them into valuable products and services. Everyone has something to offer, and our gifts just happen to be creative in some way.

In nature, apple trees produce apples, but they have no use for their own fruit. However, if they stop producing their fruit, the tree soon dies because there is no reason for the nourishment of the soil to go up the trunk and past the leaves if there is no fruit at the end of the branches.

Creative people are the same way. Use it or lose it! Keep your imagination fresh and productive, and it will continue to grow and expand. Ignore your gifts, and they will wither away and die. Please don't let that happen!

The Business of Art

The business of art is no different from any other business in the sense that a business exists to provide a product or a service for people who cannot provide it for themselves. The business of art just happens to provide creative solutions to people's needs, and as artists, we get to decide what kinds of creative solutions we want to contribute.

Conventional jobs in the world of art are sometimes difficult to come by, but the opportunities to be of service are unlimited. With every opportunity to provide something that serves the needs of others, we create an opportunity for ourselves to get paid. We get paid for solving other people's problems! That's why any business exists.

The business of art is a business of service. Perhaps your art is decorative. That includes conventional art forms, such as paintings and sculptures, as well as tattoos and jewelry for body decoration. Perhaps your artwork is more commercially oriented, such as advertising art or promotional photography. Vehicle graphics and T-shirt designs are creative embellishments that people are willing to pay for.

Whatever form of self-expression we enjoy, we must present it in a form that can be shared by others. It's only when we share our gifts with those who can benefit from them that we can expect to get paid for the work we do.

You Know You're an Artist; Now Think like a Business

As artists, we have access to unlimited imagination and some great ideas for creating things. Our imagination is a gift from the universe to us, and it is our job as artists to take what we experience in our imagination and somehow transform it into something that can be shared with others in the physical world.

It's in the sharing of our imagination that it becomes possible for us to earn money. If we don't share what we have to offer, there's no way we can get paid for keeping it to ourselves. We must do something for others if we want them to pay us.

When we have taken an idea from our imagination and transformed it into something more tangible, at that point we have developed a product or service that we can offer to the marketplace, and we are ready to enter the business world.

In order to stay in business, we need to continually develop more products. That's usually not a problem for artists because we have more imagination than a single lifetime will allow us to produce. It's great to have that unlimited supply of raw imagination available. We just need to learn how to tap into it and make use of it, and that can be a lot of fun too!

Creative people love to experiment and try new things, and the public loves to have new things. If there's an opportunity to feed that natural hunger for new things with my talent, I'll have an opportunity to turn my talent into money. Earning money is the result of satisfying the needs of others.

A business exists to provide a product or a service to people who cannot provide it for themselves. The business of art is no different from any other business in that sense. Our artwork must fulfill a need in someone else's life if we expect them to be willing to pay for it.

That leads to the question, what purpose does our artwork serve? Is it decorative or instructional, or is it perhaps meant to make a social statement or promote a particular product? When our artwork serves a purpose, we have the makings of an art-based business, and our imaginations become the unlimited resource for new material.

As professional artists, we seek that situation where our artwork satisfies our urge to create, and our service to others satisfies our bank account.

How Do I Start a Business?

Taking the first step is always the hardest. We don't know where to step, and we're afraid of stepping in the wrong direction. When we are just starting out, we need guidance and encouragement.

I'm not sure if there is a right way to start a business, but there's more than one way to do it. There have been many documented cases of successful businesses and entire industries that succeeded in spite of the fact that no one really knew what they were doing when they started out. They figured things out along the way. They had a sense of what they wanted to do, and nothing stopped them.

Having an idea or vision of what we want to achieve is essential when we are just starting out. That vision becomes the compass that points us in the right direction. Staying flexible and open to change is also essential. No one has all the answers when they're just beginning, and things keep changing rapidly once we get going. Thinking on our feet is a skill we develop and use every day.

Now let's get down to the basics of starting a business, in particular, an art-based business. Every successful business serves a purpose by providing a product or service that people value. The first question we must ask ourselves is, what product or service do *I* enjoy providing? Am I an illustrator or more of a sculptor? Would I enjoy being an interior decorator? Tattoos and designing digital games are big markets for creative expression. Where do I find my passion? Start there!

The best starting position is to acknowledge what we enjoy doing the most. Finding our passion and pursuing our own sense of fulfillment is the only way we can lead a satisfying and fulfilling life. Once that's established, the question becomes "How can my passion serve the needs of others?"

People only spend money on things that they value. If we want to earn money with our talents, we must find ways to make them valuable to the marketplace. What can people do with our artwork? How does it make them feel?

The question always remains, how can other people find value in the work that I enjoy doing? When we answer that question, we have the foundation for a successful business.

The First Step in Marketing Your Talent Is to Print a Business Card

Assuming you have created some artwork, and you have something to sell, the next step is to print a business card. This is a simple step toward declaring to the world that you have something to offer. A business card tells the world who you are, what you are offering, and how they can contact you.

Printing a business card has the effect on you of declaring to yourself that you are a businessperson. Seeing yourself as a businessperson is more than seeing yourself as an artist. To make money, you must be both. Your first business card expands your self-image from simply knowing that you have talent to declaring that you are a businessperson with something to offer in the marketplace!

Another thing to do when you're just starting out is to set up a Facebook business page. If you already have a Facebook page, then creating a business profile would be your next step.

Setting up your personal website would come after that. With today's point and click technology, most websites can be a do-it-yourself project, but help is always available. When you control your own website, you can keep it up to date and direct people to it. Your website is where you can display your current projects, and you can send and receive comments from the public.

Facebook is a "share" platform, and Google is a "search" platform. It's good to use both or similar platforms to display your work. When people know what they're looking for, they search for it on Google.

When people see something they like, they share it on Facebook. Instagram and Pinterest are similar share platforms, and they are easy to use.

Making effective use of social media, along with conventional marketing methods, will help people find you and your products when they are looking for them.

Bloom Where You're Planted

Bloom where you're planted and start where you can do the most good!

Starting where you are at is the *only* place you can start. Wishing that you were in a different situation will not change where you're at right now; however, the desire for change can become the goal to get from where you're at right now to where you really want to be.

If you're just starting out as an artist and you plan to do it professionally (meaning you want to earn a living with your art), please realize that people only pay for things that serve a purpose in their lives. As pretty as your art may be, or as dazzling and unusual as you might make it, people do not pay for things unless it benefits them in some way.

When your talent blossoms into something that serves the needs of others, like the fragrance of a flower, you will attract the attention of those who want what you have to offer, and your influence can affect the world when you share it with others.

Every Job Is Your Reputation

In the world of art and entertainment, fame and fortune are great motivators for many of us. We love the attention, the glitter, and the financial rewards. But when it comes to our career goals, it all starts with the desire to express ourselves. Once we find a way to do that, we build a reputation for ourselves by doing the kind of work and the quality of work we want to be remembered for.

When it comes to creating a business with our talents, it all boils down to establishing a reputation in the marketplace. Fame can come and go, and it can be bought with enough advertising dollars, but when it comes to surviving in the long run, it's our reputation that will build our future.

Reputations are built over time, and they're built with consistency. There's a difference between a promotion, which is a short-term activity, and branding, which is an act of developing a long-term image for ourselves. A promotion is a quick attention getter, designed to sell something within a certain period of time.

Promotions have an expiration date, while branding builds your reputation, and reputations never expire.

Plan for Your Legacy, Not
Just for Survival

For those of us who want to make a difference in the world, our legacy becomes the focus of our attention. Leaving a legacy goes along with building our reputation. What will I leave behind? What will people write on my tombstone? What would I write on my own tombstone?

These are not scary or morbid thoughts to spend our time on, but rather, they are motivating exercises that will increase the value we place on our time and efforts. We need to ask ourselves, what effect do I want my work to have on the world today, and how will my work affect the world in the future?

Write down the answer and post it where you can see it every day. Constantly seeing the goal or mission in a written statement helps to keep our attention focused on why we do the things we choose to do.

In the world of art, there are many examples of people who are famous because they changed the way we look at things. We have Picasso with cubism, Salvador Dali with his melting clocks, Andy Warhol with screen-printed images, and others who opened us up to different ways to look at things. What effect do you want your work to have on this planet after you leave?

Trying to be different just for the sake of being different is not the answer. Each of us already have unique differences built into our personal systems. All we have to do is develop those qualities into something of value to others and express them in a way that can be shared with the world.

That requires going on a self-discovery journey and sharing what you discover about yourself in some creative form. There is no competition to being yourself; there is only the process of revealing it to the world.

If You Harvest the Crop the Same Day You Plant Seeds, Chances Are Good You're Just Harvesting Weeds

It takes time to develop a business, and it takes time to build a reputation. It's helpful to recognize the process and have patience with it. A quality reputation is developed over time with consistency and the practice of continually improving our products and services.

Everything starts out small, even if it's a big idea or a monumental project. As a seed, the idea bears little physical resemblance to the end result, but within that tiny seed is the beginning of something great if we let it unfold in its natural way.

To be able to survive, everything requires a supportive environment that will nourish it. Just like the farmer in the natural world of planting seeds and harvesting the results, there is a lot of support work that's needed to keep a dream alive. A healthy return on our emotional investment depends on constant vigilance against the weeds of other people's negativity and our own complacency and neglect.

As an idea develops, it takes on a life of its own, and it gets nourishment and support from its surrounding environment. The idea will go through the necessary modifications and grow just like any other living thing as it goes through its infancy, then its adolescence, and on into maturity and fruition.

By understanding the process, we avoid the get-rich-quick schemes and focus on our long-term reputation and the long-term effects our work will have on our community and the planet.

Competition versus Creativity

Creativity is based on being resourceful and imaginative, while competition is based on comparison and judgment. To create something, you simply have to blend things into new patterns and combinations. Creativity is experimentation with curiosity, and there's no need for judgment or comparison about the results. The creative process has its own rewards.

Competition, on the other hand, is based on comparison of one thing with the value of something else. *In self-expression, there can be no competition!* No one expresses themselves in the same way or for the same reasons. From the perspective of motivation, we all have our own reasons for expressing ourselves the way we do.

Competition can be found in the marketplace, as the people in the marketplace have to make the choice about where they will spend their money. In the marketplace, the products compete for the attention of the buyers, but from the artist's perspective, the motivation to create the product in the first place remains personal.

From the creative side, there is only the motivation to express ourselves. From the competitive side, there is always the need to compare ourselves with what someone else has done. Comparing what we do to what others are doing leads us to an ego-based sense of superiority or inferiority.

Comparing ourselves to others is a form of competition. However, comparison is competing with results, not with whatever is motivating those results. As Neville, a great philosopher, wrote, "There is no opponent in the game of life, there is only the goal."

That's a wonderful approach to why we do the things we do, because it's based on what we personally want to give and receive, without comparing ourselves to others.

Compliments Are Great, but Money Is Better

When it comes to having talent and wanting to earn a living with it, regardless of what that talent may be, it needs to be encouraged. We all need encouragement along the way to becoming ourselves.

For art students and young entrepreneurs, compliments play an important role in supporting the arts, by supporting the very heart of the artist. While compliments nourish the creative spirit, money will nourish the career ambitions.

For the creative person to make a financially successful career for themselves, their talent must serve the needs of someone in the marketplace. To earn money in exchange for our talents, we must turn our gifts into something that other people value. They don't teach that in art school.

In art school, you will learn skills and techniques and how to work with a variety of materials, but unless you enroll in a commercially oriented graphics art program, the art classes won't teach you much about earning money. The key to earning money is to use your creativity to serve the needs of others.

It's only in serving the needs of others that we deserve to get paid. We're all here to serve someone in some way, whether we have a steady job with a single employer or we earn our living from one project to the next. You know you have talent; now it's time to think like a business!

Here's the key to enjoying yourself and running a successful business: if the product or service you provide involves one or more of your talents, you will probably enjoy the work you do, and you will probably do good work because you are enjoying yourself. Because you are doing good work, you will probably be paid well.

By providing a service with our talent, we can satisfy our bank account while we fulfill our creative urge for self-expression. Combining the ability to create things with the willingness to serve others is a guaranteed recipe for success.

The First Work of Art Is Yourself

We can't give what we don't have, so let's look at what we've been given to work with. We can always make things better, but we need to start someplace.

Let's start at the source, the heart of the artist. Ideas start in the imagination as an image of some kind, and once we get that image clearly focused in our mind, it fires up our emotional desire to bring that image to life. Once that image excites our passions, our passion takes over and we become inspired! The idea takes on a life of its own, as it wants us to bring it into a physical reality.

We need to work on ourselves to figure things out. We need to learn new skills and work with new materials. We must study whatever is necessary, and we need to learn from a variety of people along the way. For the inquisitive spirit, this is a lot of fun, and learning new things can be its own reward.

Artists love to learn and do new things. Repetition is not creative. As the artist, we are the first thing that needs to grow. The completed project will be an extension of our imagination and skills. It is only by working on our own selves that we can have the effect we want to have on the world around us.

The Peddler and the Salesman

There's a big difference between being a peddler and being a salesperson. A peddler tries to get rid of whatever they have, while a salesperson does their best to connect their client with the best solution for *their* needs. A salesperson becomes an integral part of another person's business as they become the connecting link between the client and the products or materials that are available.

A salesperson gets into a relationship first and sells products later. Salespeople are servants. They care about the relationship and the success of their client. A good salesperson must be reliable and willing to go the extra mile when the client needs a particular item or gets into a time crunch. By putting the client first, the salesperson comes out ahead.

While a salesperson may work for a specific company and promote a certain product, they generally remain an independent sort of person, setting their sales goals and working their own hours. As long as they make their quotas and receive their commissions, everyone is happy.

A peddler is not into relationships. The peddler just wants to make a quick buck, get the money, and probably never be seen again. A peddler does not plan to do any follow-up or future business with you. We do not want to do business with peddlers, and we certainly don't want to be one ourselves.

We are all salespeople at one time or another in our lives. We must sell someone on the idea of hiring us for a job or going out on a date with us. We must present ourselves as the best solution for whatever problem we are offering to solve.

We all have something to offer, whether it's our own products or something that we are promoting for others. When it comes to making money, success lies in meeting the needs of the marketplace by being a servant, not just a peddler.

The Rules of Wealth Are Simple:
Find a Need and Fill It

For the most part, we all want to have more money. We also want to enjoy every day of our lives. Looking at it from the opposite perspective, nobody wants to have less money, and no one wants to go to a job they don't like. Recognizing ourselves first and foremost as creative people with a desire to do something meaningful with our talent, we need to clarify within ourselves what kinds of things we enjoy doing or creating. It starts with us knowing what we want to offer.

We must find a need for the kind of products or services we offer, or we can adapt our products and services to meet the needs that we see in the marketplace. At this point, it becomes our creative responsibility to ask, "How may I serve?" We can't expect people to give us money for the things that we enjoy doing unless they are receiving something of value in return.

If we enjoy making jewelry, there's a need in the marketplace for everything from wedding rings to body piercing. If we enjoy working with paint, there's unlimited subject matter and a wide variety of materials to work with, and there are people who will buy it. For those of us who enjoy illustrations, there's everything from books to tattoos. If digital graphics and designing games are your thing, the field is wide open for you.

If you're more service oriented than product oriented, there are interior decorators and consulting services that serve department stores and the convention industry with promotional showroom displays. It all requires creative imagination and a degree of specialized skill. If you enjoy doing it, you can find a way to get paid to do it.

By shaping the most pleasant elements of your talents into the kinds of things and services that people value, you create an opportunity for yourself to satisfy your creative spirit and your bank account at the same time!

The Best Investment You Can Make

Investing in your talents is the best investment you can make! Physical things wear out with use, but talents expand and become sharper. The more we use our talents, the more talent we will have!

We are all here to serve others in some way, and as creative people, regardless of what our talent may be, we have been given a unique gift that we can share with the world. Our challenge is to find a way to package it and present it to the marketplace.

You know you have a unique gift or talent of some sort, but the big question is, what do you want to do with it? I'll always encourage you to use it! Use it or lose it! That's the way it goes. When we use our talents, everybody wins. We grow more imaginative and skillful, and the world benefits from the gifts that only we can offer.

Six Words That Lead to Success

What can I do for you?

In those six words lie the key to any business or individual who wants to move up in life. In our society, we get paid in proportion to the value of the service or product we provide to others. To increase our wealth, we simply need to find ways to increase the *value* of the work we do.

We don't necessarily have to work harder or put in more hours; we simply have to serve a greater need that the public is willing to pay for. That's working smarter, not harder.

Find a need and fill it! That is the key to creating wealth. Those six words are the same as "What can I do for you?" When we do something that serves the needs of others, that's when we deserve to receive compensation. When someone pays us for our work, we are not being compensated for our time, but rather, we are being compensated for *the value* of whatever we accomplish during the time that we are being paid. The value of the work being done determines the difference between the fifteen-dollar-an-hour paycheck and the hundred-dollar-an-hour paycheck. The time someone puts into the job is the same, but the value and the compensation can vary widely.

Our time is our most precious commodity. It can't be replaced! How we spend our time determines what we receive in return. It's up to us to set our own standards of excellence and expectations. The universe has a way of giving back to us in proportion to what is being given.

I Don't Want to Be a "Commercial" Artist. Then Again, Maybe I Do!

As a graduate of the University of Wisconsin with a degree in art, I look back on some of our discussions about "pure art" and selling out to "commercialism." Commercial art was meant for the advertising industry, and pure art was meant to be found in art museums and private collections.

We were expected to choose between being "real" artists who only do pure art and being some kind of "commercial prostitute" who sells their creative soul just to make a buck. However, it dawned on me that if we are currently employed in a job that does not require the use of any of our talents, then we are already selling out our creative soul, just to make a buck!

I remember, back in art school, we were laughing at the thought that if we ever wanted to make money, we could always paint a landscape or a seascape. We would laugh at the idea that we would see our artwork selling in department stores rather than art galleries.

It's true that we can make good money creating popular subject matter for the general public, but it's also true that we can earn very good money by specializing in specific areas of business, such as serving the youth market, focusing on corporate convention displays, and so on. I've been paid to do custom painting on motorcycles and pinstriping on automobiles. It's all various forms of artwork, and it can all be fun and profitable. If it provides a service to others, it's an opportunity to get paid.

We are all here to serve others in some way, and our talent can be our unique way of doing that. The career we choose becomes our gift to the world. The *only* thing we have to offer is our time, and we must choose to spend our time wisely because it can't be replaced!

If we want to earn money with our talents, we will have to engage in commerce. The root word of commercialism is *commerce*, meaning the exchange of goods for money. Artists survive by getting commissions or requests for specific artwork. If we want to make money, we want those commissions. We want to engage in commerce. We want to be commercial artists at some level.

We can be proud of the work we do, and we can be proud of the money we earn as a result of the service we provide. Money is the reward for a job well done, and satisfaction is the reward for a life well lived. We want the best of both!

Artists Love Expression.
The Marketplace Wants Value.
Now What?

Artists always want to express themselves in meaningful or playful ways. We hope that other people will love our work, and we hope someone will want to buy it, or at least tell us it's nice. Compliments can go a long way in encouraging us to continue our creative lifestyle, but money can go even further!

The marketplace wants value. People are willing to pay for things that they value and find useful in some way. Value is found in the purpose something serves in someone's life. It may be educational, emotional, useful, or perhaps it's a gift for someone else, but it serves the purpose of filling someone's need in some way. If you want your talent to sell, think purpose and *create value for others* with your gift.

Being paid to do something is very encouraging. That's why people show up for work every day. Being paid for doing something that we love would be a dream come true for most people. Too often, people look outside of themselves for ways to make money, but I'm here to tell you that the search for wealth starts from within. What do you have to offer?

Personal success is achieved by offering our unique skills and abilities to people who can't do what we do. The things that we enjoy doing the most are the things that we should be sharing with the world. If our job involves one or more of our talents, we will probably enjoy the work we do, and we will probably do good work because we are enjoying ourselves. We will probably be paid well because we are doing good work. We just need to let the world know what we have to offer.

Since talents expand with use, the more we use our talents, the more talents we will develop. Investing in our talents is the best investment we can make. The more good we can give, the more good we can receive in return.

We've all heard the phrase "the rich get richer, and the poor get poorer," and it's a fact. Actually, the poor don't get poorer; they just get left behind, sitting on the sidelines, wishing that somehow their life would improve but not realizing that it's up to them to develop their personal gifts and skills.

The same laws of success apply to everyone. We get out of life what we put into it. What goes around comes around, and we reap what we sow. It's all saying the same thing; give *and you shall receive!*

There's Always a Market for Those Who Can Serve

We don't get paid for having talent, but people will pay for things that add value to their lives. As artists, our talents can serve the needs of many markets, from digital game designs to the traditional high-end galleries and private collections. In between, there's illustrators, cartoonists, and T-shirt artists, along with a million other niche markets.

There's a lot of room for artists in the advertising and interior decorating business, as well as in the screen-printing industry, the tattoo industry, the jewelry business, and so forth. If a tattoo or a piece of jewelry serves a purpose or represents something meaningful to someone, there's money to be made if you have the skills to do the job.

The point is, if your artwork can serve a purpose in someone else's life, people will be willing to pay you to satisfy that need. Artwork that promotes something serves a particular purpose. Artwork that decorates a wall serves a purpose with the impression it makes on the area, whether it's meant for a baby's room or an office lobby. Artwork on a T-shirt takes on significance for the person who wears it, and jewelry has a way of making its own statement, depending on what it is and how it's worn.

The big question is, "How can the things that I enjoy creating serve a purpose in someone else's life?" Perhaps a more productive way of saying it would be, "What changes do I have to make in my way of thinking in order to serve the needs of the marketplace?"

Regardless of how we are earning a living now, we are being paid according to the value that other people place on our service. To increase our personal wealth, we must find ways to increase the value of what we offer and then manage the returns wisely.

When we think of our artwork as our way of serving others, we elevate ourselves to the level of being a business, recognizing that our skills have value to the community we live in.

We're Known by the Company We Keep

Everyone has a support system. The question is, what is it supporting us in?

For most of us, our first support system was our family, then the neighborhood we grew up in, then our childhood playmates and our early schooling, and so on. These elements became the platform that we built everything else on. Our early-childhood experiences and relationships became our unconscious partners in our personal development, and it all influenced the direction our lives have taken.

As children, we don't question much about what's happening around us. We just absorb it like a sponge, unconsciously assuming everything in our experience is the reality of the entire world. Since it's our only experience, it's the only reality we have, and we begin to build our dreams and beliefs about ourselves and our place in the world on that foundation.

If we stay in our childhood environment, it will continue to support us in being a part of that world. However, if we want to leave our childhood environment, we will need to find a new support system that will help us get to where we want to be. That system may be a form of higher education, joining the work force and getting on-the-job training, enlisting in the military, getting married, or aligning our thoughts with a new business partner.

As we rise, fall, or settle somewhere in between, we will find ourselves surrounded by like-minded people. It's that "birds of a feather sticking together" thing. Like-minded people have a way of finding each other. If we're not comfortable in a certain group or environment, we will either adjust ourselves to fit into their way of thinking, or we will look for a more supportive group somewhere else. The decisions we make in that regard will depend on our self-image and our dreams for our future. If we follow the crowd, we will fit in with the crowd. If we go our separate ways, we will meet others along the path. While most people will pass by without much effect on our life, a few will become influential to our way of thinking. As we journey through life, we will see ourselves in the faces of those we surround ourselves with.

It all starts with us, and by being the person we want to hang around with, we become the person others want to hang around with too. We get to know ourselves by the company we keep.

The Doors of Opportunity
Continue to Open

The doors of opportunity continue to open for those who are ready and willing to walk through them. As a business, we get paid when we provide a service to others. Since the opportunities to be of service are unlimited, the opportunities to earn a creative living are also unlimited. The key is to recognize the opportunity to serve and not wait to be told what must be done.

It all starts with you. What is your favorite form of creative self-expression? What do you have to offer? What do you enjoy doing, or what is it that you want to say? Whatever it is, that becomes your gift to the world!

No opportunity is lost. It is simply passed on to the next available person. If the opportunity is there, and you can see it as an opportunity instead of a problem, you have a chance to solve a problem that people are willing to pay for. Every problem requires a solution, and every solution offers the possibility of being paid in proportion to the value of the service provided.

Solution-oriented people tend to move ahead in life, sometimes by themselves, but more often they succeed as a team, working with the help of others. Thomas Edison said his greatest accomplishment was to bring the right people together. His many inventions were the result of having the right people collaborating and working as a team. While Edison gets the credit, he didn't do all the work by himself. No one does.

No sense of accomplishment comes without overcoming a challenge. The creative person is challenged with the job of bringing intangible things out of the imagination and transforming those ideas into the physical world, where they can be shared and experienced by others.

It is the artist's job to take raw ideas from the mental realm and transform them into products and experiences that can be shared in the physical world.

Not All Artwork Is Found in Galleries

Not all artwork is found in galleries. In fact, very little of it is. Art galleries are niche markets all their own. They provide a type of art to a specific type of buyer, and it seems that most art schools focus their teaching methods on this market.

For the artists who want to earn a living with their talents, the whole world is their potential market. The business of art is no different from any other business in the sense that a business exists to provide a product or a service to people who cannot provide it for themselves.

If you want to earn money with your art, you must be willing to exchange your talent for cash. You must see your product or service as a *commodity* that has value.

As businesspeople, we must ask ourselves, "What purpose do I want this business to serve? What product or service do I want to provide with my talent?" The product or service we provide will be a creative solution to someone else's need. It may look like a painting, or it may look like a sculpture. It may take the form of a design or a consulting service, but whatever it is, it will have to serve a purpose in someone's life, or it won't be something people will pay for.

If we want to make money, we must recognize the needs of the marketplace and then shape our talents to meet those needs. There's a market for creative things at every level of the financial spectrum, from T-shirts and advertising to top-level art galleries. Artists are needed in developing new digital games, and there's the screen-printing industry, the tattoo and jewelry business, and on and on. Art is literally everywhere we look.

Your unique style of creativity will lead you to your own niche, and all you have to do is fill it!

We Never Graduate from a Lifetime of Learning

We never graduate from the process of learning new things. There are always new things to discover and things we can develop further, and there are infinitely more things to create for ourselves and others.

As artists, we are constantly challenged to find new ways of looking at things, both in the physical world and in our personal and spiritual lives. We learn by doing, and we challenge ourselves to try new things. We will never run out of new things to try!

Once we learn a skill, such as drawing and coloring, we then learn other skills, such as perspective and shading. There's always more to add to our encyclopedia of skills, and the creative part of us loves the challenge! Once we've mastered the basic techniques and we have something to offer to the public, we're ready to earn some money. For this, we will need to learn another skill called marketing.

It takes courage to put our best work out there and hope that somebody will like it. It hurts to be laughed at, or perhaps even worse, to be completely ignored. Why bother? Does anybody care? Yes! Everybody cares ... *about themselves*!

We care about ourselves! We *want* to create the art! We *want* to express ourselves! We are motivated by our own self-interests, and so is everybody else! It's only when we serve the needs of others with our talents that we can convert our talent into cash. That's where marketing comes in.

Learning to serve the needs of others is the key to making money. We all have to work for someone in some fashion in order to get paid, so we might as well use our unique gifts as our way of serving our community.

The big question becomes, "What do people want that I enjoy giving?" A similar way to ask the same question would be, "What things do I enjoy doing that can be done in a way that benefits others?"

That leads to the question of what purpose do we want our artwork to serve? Is our artwork meant to be used as decoration on a wall or as a tattoo on someone's body? Is our artwork more like jewelry, symbolizing something sacred or meaningful?

Your talent may be more inclined toward doing sophisticated gallery artwork, or perhaps your work is meant to be purchased as an investment for the future value it might bring. Perhaps your style is more inclined toward temporary things, such as seasonal greeting cards, wearable T-shirt designs, and short-term promotional materials.

As an artist, there's money to be made doing many kinds of artwork. The money lies in satisfying a purpose in the buyer's mind. Can your artwork serve as a gift item for someone else? Does it promote something? Is it a documentary photograph or political/ social cartoon or commentary? Tattoos and jewelry are personalized items that decorate the body to make a personal statement.

These are all good questions we need to ask ourselves, and learning to answer them will give us more clarity in marketing our passion to others. When our artwork serves a purpose in someone else's life, they will be willing to pay for it.

The Grass Always Looks Greener on the Other Side of the Fence

Have you ever found yourself frustrated and perhaps even angry that the boss is making all the money while you're doing all the work? When we're just starting our career, what we learn is more important than what we earn. The money will come, and the money will go, but the lessons are ours to keep.

I almost always encourage creative people to run their own businesses, but when we're just getting started, we need to get some on-the-job experience. When starting a new job, the first thing we need to learn is the job expectations. Then we need to learn how to operate any special equipment that we'll be using. Finally, perhaps the most challenging task of all may be figuring out how to fit into the prevailing social order, as we figure out the community work ethic and learn the personalities of our fellow employees.

Once we prove we have the basic experience and skills needed to get hired, everything from then on will consist of expanding our skills and gaining more experience from the various projects we work on.

When we run our own operation, we are responsible for a lot of things, and we are responsible to a lot of people. As an employee, we are usually responsible to only one person, and that is our supervisor. This may be the owner of the company or a midlevel manager. Either way, we would be working for someone, and we would be required to meet their expectations.

We all need to serve someone in order to get paid. That's how the system works. Regardless of what our career might be, we get compensated for our time, based on how much the marketplace values our services. The question becomes, who do we want to work for, a steady employer or a series of individual clients?

Some of the benefits of being an employee are that the company we work for is supplying us with the project, and we did not have to spend any of our own money on advertising to get the job for ourselves. The company is providing a place to do the work that has proper lighting and year-round temperature control, and they supply the tools and the materials that are needed to do the job.

As artists, we get the fun job of doing the actual work. All that other stuff needs to be handled first, before anyone gets to work on it. As a bonus for the employee, every job is an opportunity to learn something, so having a job is like getting paid to go to school!

Don't ever think that the guy in the office isn't doing his share of the work. He spent his money when he advertised the business that got the customer to come through the door. The owner is paying rent for the shop space, and he's paying for the electricity, and very likely he's making payments on the equipment that's being used to do the job.

Oftentimes, a business owner doesn't want to lose good employees, so they will pay their employees during slow times without taking a paycheck for themselves. The owner of a business takes on a lot more responsibility than an employee ever deals with, so while the grass may look greener on the other side of the fence, there's a lot more to it than meets the eye.

PART 2

General

Observations

PART 2

General
Observing

What Is the Carrot That
Moves You Forward?

What motivates you? What do you want? What makes you get up in the morning and want to accomplish something? Make a list of your greatest want-tos and prioritize them into levels of importance. There will be things that you want to have, things that you want to do, and things that you want to be.

Everything starts with desire, from the simplest desire to be more comfortable to the greatest desire to build an empire or put a man on the moon. Most of our desires will fall somewhere in between those extremes.

We all want money. Some want more, and others are satisfied with less, but we all want enough money to live comfortably. We all want health. We often take our health for granted until it gives us problems. We can't function at our best without good health.

We all want love. I want love, and you want to be loved. We want to give it, and we want to receive it. It's a universal desire that fits in with our desire to belong to something. We have a universal desire to be a part of something bigger than ourselves. Solitary confinement or the feeling of separation is a painful experience.

Lastly, we want our lives to be meaningful on some level. If we feel that our life has no meaning or that the work we do doesn't matter, it gets depressing. We want to live meaningful lives. We want our work to be more than just a paycheck. As creative beings, we want to make a difference. We want our time on earth to show some kind of value for how we spent it.

Make a list now of the things that are important to you. You must write them down so you can see the list grow and change as you mature. The list won't forget, but you will, so write down your priorities somewhere where you can see them. Your life will go in the direction of your thoughts. Always keep your goals at the forefront of your awareness.

It will be fun to look back at your dreams five years from now.

Discovering Our Purpose

A strong sense of purpose in life is essential for being able to feel satisfied and fulfilled. It's hard to feel satisfied if we're not sure of what we're trying to accomplish. A strong sense of purpose defines the mission that determines the direction our entire life will go in.

We find our purpose in the things that bring us pleasure. The things that we enjoy doing the most, are the things we should be doing for others. If we find pleasure in working with technology, that's an indication that that may be where we can do the most good. If we find pleasure in physical activities, that's a sign that we might do well helping others find a similar joy. Sharing our passion with the world is exciting! The challenge is to figure out the best way to do it.

The overall goal is to find pleasure and fulfillment for ourselves. We want to live a complete and satisfying life. We do this by serving the needs of others with our unique gifts and talents. We can't give what we don't have, so let's look at what we *do* have to offer. We start with the best of whatever we can do at this moment, and we can always make improvements as we move along.

In planning our career goals, we are searching for personal fulfillment, not sacrifice. The key to happiness and success is to do things for others in a way that brings us pleasure. We will gladly sacrifice things with a lower priority in favor of things that bring us a greater sense of satisfaction or fulfillment. Those smaller sacrifices lead to a greater sense of accomplishment.

Fulfilling our purpose creates a win-win situation, where we get the joy and pleasure of working with our talents, and the world gets the benefit of all that we have to offer.

Are You Purpose or Paycheck Oriented?

There's a difference between a paycheck-oriented worker and a purpose-oriented worker. A purpose-oriented worker knows *why* something is being done and understands the mission of the project, while a paycheck-oriented worker only knows what needs to be done in order to keep their job.

It's easier to put our best effort into making things happen if we understand the mission or purpose of the work we are doing. It helps us to work toward the perfect end result if we understand what the end result looks like or what it's meant to accomplish.

The paycheck-oriented employee needs to be told what to do, because they don't have the end result in mind. They don't see the big picture. Their focus is more on their personal paycheck than on the company's mission.

If we're just working for a paycheck, it's easier to focus on the time clock and to think about our personal plans for the weekend than it is to take pride in the work we are doing at the moment.

The purpose-oriented person understands the mission of the project and does not need to be told what to do. They see what needs to happen in order to reach the preferred end result, and they proceed to do what needs to be done in order to make that happen. Purpose-oriented people are self-motivated and have a clear direction or goal for their life. Every project is another stepping stone toward their personal success.

We may not always have a job, but we always have a purpose. If we know what our purpose is, then our job is to fulfill our purpose!

We're Only as Old as Our Newest Ideas

We're only as old as our newest ideas, and we're only as young as our oldest beliefs. We think with our ideas, and we act on our beliefs. As humans, our thoughts show up in the physical world through our beliefs and the actions that follow. We all act on our beliefs, whether they are based on something that is true and accurate or on something that is inaccurate or mistaken. If we believe it, we will act accordingly.

With today's rapidly changing environment and socially engaging technologies, learning new things is necessary for practical reasons as well as for maintaining a healthy, functioning brain. Keeping the brain healthy requires us to challenge old thoughts and beliefs, much like working out at the gym requires using challenging weights and difficult exercises.

We must challenge ourselves to think in new ways just to keep up with this ever-changing moment in time. If there's no exercise for the body or the brain, the muscles or the thought processes become stiff, and they lose their natural flexibility. As always, we must use it, or we will lose it.

If we took away our man-made contraptions like clocks and calendars, and we simply lived in the moment of now, we would have no concept of aging. We would have our memories to draw from past experiences, and we could imagine a future and make plans for ourselves, but there would be no concept of being too young or too old for something. There would only be an appropriate behavior for the moment at hand.

Living in the now, or living in this moment, liberates us from the past, and it provides an open page for the future that is yet to be written.

I Know the Answers;
I Just Never Asked the Questions

We are all smarter than we realize, but sometimes it takes something outside of ourselves to help us realize that. That's one of the reasons I love teaching. Students ask questions I would never ask on my own, yet when I put a little thought into it, I realize I know the answer, and I've known the answer all along, but I would not have asked that particular question. I would not have realized that I knew something unless an outside force had caused my thinking to go in that direction.

And so it goes. We look for outside forces that will cause us to think and learn new things, or, to say it more accurately, we seek things that will cause us to be aware of what some part of us already knows. We increase our own self-awareness when we realize that our lives go deeper than our present level of knowledge.

As human beings, most of us are aware that there is more to life than meets the eye. There's something that is driving us forward as a species, and as individuals, we are playing a part in that eternal process. There's something that causes us to contemplate our future, to think about our destiny, and to plan for our eventual demise.

We recognize the pattern, and we know that we are participants in that pattern. Each of us is somewhere in that process, experiencing whatever it is that's appropriate for us to learn at this time.

When we ask questions, we discover things. One of the things we discover is that we knew the answers all along; we just never asked the questions. In so many situations, we realize that we already have the knowledge; we only need to increase our awareness of how smart we really are.

The Wizard of Oz Revisited

I think most of us are familiar with the story of *The Wizard of Oz*. As a quick recap, let me review the basic storyline for you here. There are four main characters in the story, Dorothy, the Scarecrow, the Tin Man, and the Cowardly Lion.

The story begins with a tornado forcing everyone to take shelter, but Dorothy gets hit on the head from a flying window and passes out. She has a dream, and in this dream, she wants to get back to her home in Kansas. She is told to "follow the yellow brick road," which leads to the land of Oz, and there, the Wizard could help her.

So, she sets out on her journey, and she meets the Scarecrow, who is upset because he doesn't have a brain. Dorothy tells him about the Wizard, and they set out together to see if they can find him. They come upon the Tin Man, who is crying because he's hollow inside and doesn't have a heart. The three of them go on their journey toward Oz, when a lion jumps out in front of them, but it's more funny than scary. The lion is sad because he has no courage, and he can't frighten anyone. The three friends convince the Cowardly Lion to join them on their journey to Oz. Perhaps the Wizard could help him too.

Along their journey, they meet up with the Wicked Witch of the West, who captures Dorothy and imprisons her in a dungeon. The Scarecrow convinces the lion to dress up as one of the flying monkey guards and march into the castle with them. He gets into the castle, and he opens the gate. The Tin Man uses his ax to free Dorothy, and they continue their journey to Oz.

They arrive at the Wizard's castle, only to find out that the Wizard is a fake! He's just a man behind the curtain, making a lot of smoke and noise. However, he points out that they never needed him anyway, because they already had everything they were looking for.

The Scarecrow had the intelligence to figure out how to rescue Dorothy. The lion had the courage to enter the castle. The Tin Man was crying when they met him, and he couldn't cry if he didn't have a heart! Dorothy wanted to get back home to Kansas, but she was always in her home. She had only been dreaming that she was lost.

The Wizard of Oz is our story. We each have a brain like the Scarecrow, and we can use it to solve problems. Like the Tin Man, we all have a heart that enables us to express our feelings. Like the lion, we have the courage to do what needs to be done when the challenges arrive, and like Dorothy, we are always where we belong. We just need to realize it!

Thinking with Imagination, Leaving Out the Limitations

Einstein once said something to the effect of, knowledge is limited to what we know, while imagination has no limits.

By living with imagination, we open ourselves up to believing that anything is possible. Dreams, goals, and wishes are imaginary things that drive us forward in our daily activities. They each contain a vision, an imaginary picture of something that isn't physical or tangible at this moment.

As we imagine something that could be different in our daily life, we tend to go in the direction of that imagined vision. "As you believe, so shall it be" is the law of creation. Our beliefs will create our experiences.

Believing in what we imagine is what has gotten us everything we have so far, so the key to experiencing something different in our lives is to believe something different to be true.

If we choose to believe in our limitations, we will experience them as our reality. They may not be real for anyone else, but they will be very real for us. As Richard Bach says in his book *Illusions*, "Argue for your limitations, and they're yours to keep!"

I'll stay focused on Einstein's observation that imagination has no limitations, and we'll see where it goes from there!

You Won't Find Your Purpose
in the Help Wanted Ads

You may not always have a job, but you always have a purpose. If you know what your purpose is, then your job is to fulfill your purpose.

We find our purpose in the things that excite us and spark our curiosity, things we consider fun and enjoyable. In the pleasant feelings we get from those subjects lie the keys to living a fulfilling and satisfying life.

If we follow our sense of purpose and see where it leads, we will be led on a magnificent adventure that will be unique to each of us. On this adventure, we will meet the most interesting people, and our days will be filled with meaningful experiences.

No two people have the same journey to travel, and no two people have the same message to give. No two people have the same lessons to learn, nor do they have the same reasons for learning them.

The things we enjoy doing the most are the things we should be doing for others. Those things are our specialties. Those are the things we will be best at doing, because we always give our best to the things we love the most.

You Don't Have to Be Special to Be Special to Someone

We all look up to someone, and someone is always looking up to us. We're all on a ladder of sorts as we climb on the accomplishments of those who have gone before us, and we reach down to help those who want to rise with us.

We may be traveling a path that's been built by others, or we may be finding our own way through the woods, but we will leave a path for others to follow. If someone else can do it, then we can too. If we can do it, others can learn how.

We all have our own path to follow, and we all have our own choices to make along the way. Some of the people we meet on our journey will become special to us, and by our example, we will become special to someone else as we go along our way.

If I Don't Have Confidence, Please Give Me Courage

Courage and confidence go hand in hand with success. It takes courage to try new things and to do things that we don't know how to do. Confidence is the result we get when we accomplish something we had the courage to try.

It takes courage to go where we've never been before. There's always a challenge of confronting the unknown, and the unknown is everywhere around us. The future is unknown. It takes a certain amount of courage to get out of bed every day, but with the confidence we gain by confronting our fears, we continually learn from our mistakes as well as our successes. In that process, we gain the courage to try even bigger things.

Our sense of confidence grows when we have positive experiences, and we gain encouraging reinforcement from the results. Once we recognize the process, we can control the cycle of courage that develops greater confidence, and we can watch our lives continually spiral upward toward an ever bigger and more fulfilling way of life.

I Can Show You the Path, but You Still Have to Walk the Distance

There are no shortcuts, but there's always a way to get from here to there, if we know where we want to go. Sometimes, deciding where we want to go is more difficult than actually getting there. However, once we decide on a destination, the next thing to do is to head in that direction. *Get on with it!* Committing to that first step may be the biggest challenge.

It's important to have good mentors along the way. For the lucky ones, we may have had good parents and maybe some good schooling when we were growing up. Maybe an uncle or a grandparent taught us some valuable lessons that have served us well throughout our lifetime. We all learned something from someone, and it's gotten us this far.

Having a goal or a destination is simply an excuse to go on a journey. There are no shortcuts, but we can save a lot of time along the way if we stay on the path and don't get lost.

Some say, "Follow their example and do what others have done," and others say, "Find your own way and leave a path for others to follow." I'm not sure if one way is better than the other, but the path becomes clear once the destination is defined.

Everyone has their own path to follow. It may not always be clear, but it's there, waiting to be discovered and traveled, but we will only see the path after we commit to going on the journey.

It Ain't What You've Been Given; It's What You Do with It That Matters

If you were given a ten-pound block of steel, and steel was selling for one dollar per pound, you would have something that was worth ten bucks. If you take that same block of steel and develop it into a useful tool, for the amount of work and effort you put into it, that block of steel might be transformed into something that is worth one hundred dollars. However, if you refined that block of steel into something as delicate as Swiss watch springs, that same block of steel might be worth thousands of dollars.

Our time, our talent, and our unique situation in life can be made into many different things, and the value is not determined by what we've been given to work with but by what we do with the things we've been given to work with.

The only thing we've been given is time. It's the most precious thing we have, because once it's gone, it won't come back. What we do with our time will determine what we do with our potential. We can let it sit dormant within us, or we can refine it into a skill that serves the needs of others while it provides us with a sizeable income.

It ain't what we've been given; it's what we do with it that matters.

I'm Always Happy,
but I'm Never Quite Satisfied

Being happy is a choice, and satisfaction is a feeling. They both result from the visions and beliefs we hold in our minds. We can choose to feel any way we want, and being happy is a state of mind based on *making the choice* to be happy. Happiness, anger, depression, and excitement are all feelings that result from the images we put our attention on. Everything begins in the imagination.

There are images that get us excited, and there are images that cause us to feel anger. There are images that stir the feelings of joy, hope, fear, and so on. These images live in our minds as pictures, and as artists, we can learn ways to use those pictures to express ourselves.

Pictures arouse our emotions, and our emotions motivate us to take whatever action we think is appropriate at the time. Making the choice to be happy is to make the choice to surround ourselves with happy images. "Whatsoever things are of good report, think on these things."

On the other hand, feeling satisfied is like enjoying dessert at the end of a good meal. We deserve to treat ourselves to a sweet reward when we accomplish something of value. However, if we only live on the sweet desserts, the other aspects of a healthy lifestyle tend to suffer.

The feeling of being satisfied may be our ultimate goal, but if we are always satisfied, we will become complacent, and complacency defeats our motivation. When that happens, satisfaction becomes a liability instead of a reward.

Money is the reward for a job well done, and satisfaction is the reward for a life well lived. If there's still room to grow and more of life to be enjoyed, then satisfaction can only be experienced like a sweet dessert and not as the main diet.

Divine discontent stirs the creative spirit into action, and happiness and satisfaction result when we respond appropriately.

Artists Are like Apple Trees

Apple trees produce apples, but they have no use for their own fruit. However, if the apple tree stops producing its fruit, the branches soon become brittle and the tree dies, because there is no reason for the nourishment of the soil to go up the trunk and past the leaves if there is no fruit at the end of the branches.

The apple tree produces fruit to keep itself alive, and as a result, the world benefits from its products. As artists, we produce art as a way of keeping ourselves alive, mentally and spiritually, as well as financially. Producing new art is one way to keep our imaginations fresh and vibrant.

Like the apple tree, we may not have much use for some of the artwork we produce, but we understand that it is the *process of creating something* that makes us feel most alive! Experiencing the creative process can be its own reward, as we feel our connection to something greater than ourselves while it expresses itself through us.

Apple trees don't compare themselves to other trees and then wish they were born as an orange tree, just because people drink more orange juice than apple juice. For an artist to compare their creative expression to someone else's form of expression is just as absurd.

We all have our own gifts to give, and we all have our own lessons to learn. If we use our gifts, we will learn our lessons, and life will be meaningful and rewarding in ways that only those who choose that path will know.

If we choose to play it safe, and we do not develop our unique gifts, we will find ways to earn a living and survive financially, but we will never have the experience of connecting to that creative source within us, and we will never know the satisfaction and sense of fulfillment that is meant to be ours.

Artists Live in Two Different Worlds

We all live in two different worlds, meaning we experience the world around us, and we have access to the imaginary world within us that we see when we dream or when we close our eyes and still see things. Both worlds are very real, but both worlds are very different.

The difference between those of us who think we are creative and those of us who think we aren't, is only a difference in awareness. The creative person pays attention to the images they experience when they close their eyes. Artists recognize those images as the source of their personal creative expression.

People who say they have no imagination are simply not paying attention to whatever they see when they close their eyes. Perhaps they think it doesn't matter; but when someone closes their eyes, there's still something there to see! The artist pays attention to those images.

Dreams are real! Visions are real things. Images and visions have an effect on us, and it can be powerful! The professional artist understands this and learns to use the power of the image to express their message. I could go on forever about that, but let's get back to the topic of the two worlds we live in.

There's the obvious world that we are walking around in. We call it the physical world, or the objective world. From the time we are born, up to this very moment, we absorb influences from the world around us. These experiences of color and sound, mixed with the sensations of touch and smell and taste, become the raw material of our experience of life on earth.

These experiences immediately become mental material for our brain and mind, as they instantly file into our memory of the moment. Our short-term memory helps us remember where we parked the car and how to get back home, while our long-term memories become part of who we think we are, and they influence who we become over time.

We are all creators, and we create our life experiences with our imaginations and our beliefs. The "creative" person continually imagines new ideas and new combinations of possibilities, while the "noncreative" person imagines the same images in their mind, day after day. Consequently, their world doesn't appear to change much, even though they are just as creative as anyone else; they just aren't creating any variety in their imagination. Consequently, they just keep themselves busy creating the same results over and over.

No One Is Born with Talent

No one is born with talent, but we are all born with a natural curiosity about things. We want to crawl around corners and climb up stairs. We want to learn new things, and we do dangerous things because we have no fear. If our curiosity is encouraged in some way, such as catching a moving ball, or coloring inside the lines, we will develop some skills in those areas.

Talent is simply something that has been developed into a skill. When our skill level in a particular subject rises above what is considered to be average or normal, other people recognize that level of skill as being "talented," and they put that label on us.

If someone feels that they are not talented, it is only because they do not have enough interest in the subject to develop their skills in that area. In essence, to become talented, all a person needs to do is increase their level of interest in the subject, and they will naturally pursue the skills that are associated with that subject. As the skills are mastered, the talent begins to shine through.

Talents develop with practice. *There ain't no free lunch!* Practice can be fun and enjoyable as we learn new things along the way. To be talented, we must pursue our interests to the point where we develop them into skills.

Investing in our talents is the best investment we can make! The more we use our talents, the more talent we will have. Physical things wear out with use, while talent and imagination grow stronger!

There's Nothing Artificial about Using Our Own Intelligence

Using our own intelligence involves using our own judgment and not relying on the latest state-of-the-art technology to make our decisions for us. Perhaps AI can provide some guidance and some quick answers, but it cannot make our decisions. The decisions we make are our personal responsibility, and most of our decisions are based on emotional responses to things. While artificial intelligence can figure things out in a matter of seconds, it cannot know how we feel about those things.

As human beings, we make most of our decisions based on our emotions, and then we let our intellectual abilities figure out how to achieve the results we want.

Artificial intelligence can offer up a wide variety of options in a very short period of time, but ultimately, it is our personal intelligence that has to make the decisions that affect our lives the most.

Independence versus Self-Reliance

Is there really such a thing as being "independent"? I don't think so. Independent of what? Independent of each other? That's not possible. It's more like everything is interdependent, relying on and reacting to everything that is happening around it.

Rather than being independent, I sense a universal pattern of interdependence, from the smallest cells in our bodies interacting with each other to the planets in the solar system affecting one another as they spin around in space. The sun provides the heat for the plants to grow, and the plants rely on the soil, while animal life depends on the plants, and so forth.

Self-reliance, on the other hand, is the ability for an individual to get things done by working with the interdependence of the elements. By working with whatever is available now, the self-reliant person draws the necessary elements and the right people together to create a product or a service that one individual working alone could not do.

None of us are independent. It is only by recognizing and accepting the interdependence of ourselves with everything else that we will find solutions to living together on this planet.

The Keys to Happiness and the Keys to Success

While the keys to happiness and the keys to success are very powerful, as with most truths, the principle is very simple at its core. The key to happiness is to figure out what you like to do and then find a way to get paid to do it. The key to success is that you can get paid to do anything, as long as it benefits someone else.

People don't pay us for the amount of work we do; they pay us for the amount of benefit they receive from the work we do. People pay for benefits. People are willing to pay for things that improve their lives in some way, so the question we must ask ourselves is, "How can the things I enjoy doing benefit other people?"

When we can answer that question, we set ourselves in the direction of our personal, spiritual, and financial success, based on the fulfillment of our urge to express ourselves.

For most people, life can be a dream come true when they get paid to do something that they enjoy doing. The things we enjoy doing the most are the things we should be sharing with others. We always do our best when we love the things we do.

The Real Reward for Our Efforts

The real rewards for our efforts are not found in the money we get paid for the work we do; but rather, the real rewards are found in *what we become* by the work we do.

Do we continue to learn new things, thereby becoming smarter? Do we become more creative, more caring, and more loving toward ourselves and others because of our work?

When we serve the needs of others with the gifts that we've been given, satisfying our creative spirit can lead to filling the bank account as well.

Money is the reward for a job well done, while personal fulfillment is the reward for a life well lived.

We All Start at the Beginning, Then Realize There Is No End

We all start at our own beginning, whether it's starting a business or a new project or getting into a new relationship. Everything begins at some point, but it never really ends. The experiences we go through tend to become a part of us. They go into our memory file, and we allow the effect of the experience to become part of our learning curve in life. Our minds become like an encyclopedia of collected lessons.

The lessons we learn along the way are ours to keep, and they influence us from the day we learn them until we either unlearn them or we die. With the constant and rapid changes in just about everything these days, learning new things is a way of life. For children, it's easy. They learn new things every day without realizing it. It becomes a bit more challenging for us as we age.

Throughout our lives, we have learned things that have worked well in the past, but now they don't work as well or even at all! As we age, we are forced to choose between relying on our past experience and experimenting with new ways of doing old things.

That's where the unlearning part takes place. Unlearning old beliefs that have worked over the years but no longer give me the results I want requires more energy than learning something "right" in the first place. What was right in the past may not be the right thing today.

For me, unlearning something requires the reevaluation of my priorities, and it requires a somewhat painful reckoning on my current results. At my current age of seventy-three, there are a lot of things I thought I would have done by now that I haven't gotten around to yet.

That's inspiring! Everything I haven't done yet gives me a good reason to continue getting up every day! With a childlike curiosity, I learn new things each day, and I remain an active contributor to my community.

A long time ago, I started at my beginning, and today I keep on keeping on because there is no end to learning new things!

Searching for Job Security?
Find a Need and Fill It!

In this time of rapid change in the way things are being done, job security can only be found in our willingness to serve others.

There are so many ways to make things better in this world, so there is no reason for the creative person to sit around with nothing to do. If you can't find a job, perhaps you can start your own business. Find a need and fill it!

A person gets paid in proportion to the service they give to others. We can increase our wealth by increasing the value of the service we offer to our community. We can do that by taking on more responsibility or by increasing the quality of the service we offer.

When we satisfy our need to express ourselves in a way that other people find beneficial, we have the makings of a great business, or at least the foundation for earning a good income. By expressing our talents in a way that benefits others, we have the keys to wealth and success right there in front of us.

I'll always encourage you to develop your talents with an eye for serving others. By combining the joy we find in the work we do with the willingness to serve the needs of others, we set ourselves up for financial success as well as providing ourselves with a sense of personal fulfillment.

Money is the reward for a job well done, and satisfaction is the reward for a life well lived.

Our Time Is All We Have to Offer

Our time is the only thing we have to give. Actually, time is the *only* thing that we've been given, but the problem is we just don't know how much of it is ours!

What we do with our time determines the quality of our lives, the quality of the work we do, and the gifts we give to our community, family, and employers.

Our career is our gift to the world. Choosing our career is to choose how we will spend or invest most of our time. The very thought of *spending* our time is different from the thought of *investing* our time. When we invest, we expect a return on our investment, but when we spend our time or our money, it's essentially gone.

We all begin our lives with some innate qualities, whether they are genetically or environmentally given to us. This becomes the raw material we can work with. If we are encouraged to develop our unique qualities, our lives will go in that direction. Encouragement is very helpful, and it mostly comes from our environment.

We learn useful skills and social behaviors from our environment, and then we give the results of what we have learned back to our community in the form of services and products.

Having a unique set of skills to offer and an attitude of wanting to serve others in some way creates a winning combination for living a successful life on our own terms. When we give of ourselves to the best of our abilities, we can write our own ticket to having what we want. It's the old law of what goes around comes around, or we get back what we put out.

We all find some form of employment as a way to earn a return on the investment of our time. The wonderful thing is that we get to choose what kind of employment we want to offer. By developing our gifts into products and services that other people value, we turn our time into something that benefits the community we choose to serve.

Our career is our gift to the world, and it's up to us to make it the best we can offer.

Give a Man a Fish or Teach Him How to Fish

There's an old saying that says, "If you give a man a fish, you will feed him for a day, but if you teach him how to fish, he will feed himself for a lifetime."

A similar statement is "When you teach someone something, you change their life. When you teach someone how to teach others, you can change the world!"

In this fast-paced, ever-changing world, there are those of us who are born into it and think life at this pace is normal, while there are others of us who are now living an outdated lifestyle, based on a time that wasn't so long ago. There are those of us who are caught in the middle, perhaps dogpaddling to keep up while struggling just to keep moving forward.

I confess I'm one of those who are dogpaddling to keep up with changes while I do my best to leave a legacy of good things that may serve someone in the future, long after I'm gone.

Ideas have a life of their own. Some of them tend to live on, long after the creator has passed. We still depend on some of these ancient teachings to give us guidance in today's world.

The teachings don't change, but our ability to understand them does. Our ways of looking at things change as we grow up, and our ways of socially interacting change as the world continues to mature as well.

A society is simply a gathering of people who agree to live under a certain set of rules about behavior and beliefs. As the beliefs change, the rules change, and entire societies change along with their ideas.

As an elder statesman in today's world, I look to the younger generation to show me how to make things work. The "now generation" has a different way of doing things than the way I was taught, but I believe life still operates by the same set of divine rules. You get out of life what you put into it, or you reap what you sow. Life is a mirror of what we believe to be true, and the way we look at things determines what we see.

As I continue to age, and things continually change around me, I still look for people who can teach me how to fish, rather than finding myself sitting on the sidelines, hoping someone will toss me a fish now and then.

The Four Elements of Being Human

In our desire to live a creative life, we need to address the four elements of being human. We want to establish a sense of balance among the elements. Too much of a good thing is not a good thing, and not having enough of what we need in any area of our life leaves us with a feeling of lack or inadequacy.

Let's take a quick look at each element of being human and see how they show up in our everyday lives. The first element to consider is our physical body, our actual presence on this planet. Our body is the tool or machine that carries out our mental decisions. If we mentally decide to lift our arm to answer the phone, our body responds in an appropriate manner.

The second element to consider about being human is our emotions, or how we feel about things, including ourselves. We are emotional beings, and how we feel about things determines how we respond to situations and how we treat ourselves and others. We all have been given the same set of emotions to work with at birth. We all have the capacity to feel love, joy, fear, anger, jealousy, desire, and a hundred other emotions, but what makes us appear to be different is which emotions we choose to express or repress at any given moment. People tend to react differently to the same stimulation.

Our creativity comes from wanting to express our emotions. Learning to control our emotions can be a lifelong process, like herding cats or channeling floodwaters. As artists, we learn to express our emotions through our art and various other ways.

The third element to consider about being human is the intellect. Our intellectual abilities are responsible for figuring things out and making choices. The intellect has the capacity for understanding numbers and language, and it gives us the ability to agree on time, financial values, locations, and so forth.

The fourth element of our humanity is the fact that we are alive! Life itself is an element of being human, and it expresses itself through our bodies and our minds. As long as we have the element of life actively beating our hearts and breathing our lungs, we can think with our intellect and feel with our emotions as we move our physical bodies around.

There you have it! It's a four-part description of a human being as a physical body, powered by Life itself, having the emotional capacity to feel and the intellectual ability to figure things out.

The Laws of Success Don't Work
They Only Exist. (We Do the Work!)

The laws of success exist, but they only work when we do. There's no real mystery about being successful, but first we need to define what being successful means to us. It's different for everyone, but let's assume it boils down to simply having the things we want in life.

The biggest law of success that I can think of is "what goes around comes around", or we reap what we sow. When we think about what we want to get out of life, we must first look at what we want to give, because that is the seed of what we will get back in return. Our life is no different from the farmer who intentionally sows a particular type of seed because he wants to reap a particular crop in return for his investment.

That same way of thinking applies to money and relationships and how we choose to invest our time. We need to trust that the investment of our time, talent, and emotions will give us a satisfactory return. We want to feel good about how we spend or invest our time.

In business, we not only invest financially, but we also invest our time in developing relationships with our clients. As salespeople, we nurture our relationships by being sure that our clients get what they are looking for. The return on our investment of time and caring can pay dividends for years to come.

In the area of love and personal friends, we invest our time and our emotions to build strong and trusting relationships. If we want to trust people, we need to plant the seeds of trust first. It's not important that we know we can trust others; what's important is that we know others can trust us! What we see in others, we see in ourselves. There's always something in other people that triggers a feeling that relates to something within ourselves.

There are other laws of success that deal with the quality of service, the laws of expansion, the power of belief, and so forth, but the greatest law I can think of is *the more you give, the more you will receive.*

Education Is Expensive,
but So Is Ignorance

Education can be expensive, but ignorance can cost us even more! Ignorance leads to missed opportunities and our life being lived in smaller ways than would be necessary.

Education doesn't always happen in the established schools and universities, but associating with the right people will give us the hands-on experience we need. The question becomes, what do we want to achieve, and what do we need to learn to achieve it?

Just answering those questions will be an education in itself. Very few people really know what they want. It's easy to get distracted by the glitter of get-rich-quick schemes or to get thrown off track by some well-intentioned friend who warns us of the dangers of following our dreams.

We should never take advice from someone who doesn't have what we want! If they don't have it, they can't tell us how to get it because they don't know what they're talking about. Only the people who have what we want can tell us how they got what they have. If they don't have the results we're looking for, don't take their advice, or we'll end up like them!

Role models are important, because they give us examples to follow. If they can do it, we can do it. We just have to figure out what they did. While we can learn from a role model's example, there's a difference between imitating someone and emulating someone.

Imitation is perhaps a form of flattery, but it automatically puts us in second place. By imitating someone, we're copying someone's results rather than following their process and creating our own results. By emulating someone, we follow their attitude or behavior, and in that way, we become more like them while we express our own unique ideas.

We must learn whatever we need to learn in order to be the person we want to be. The person we want to be lives inside of us, waiting to grow, mature, and bear fruit, just like the apple tree lives inside of the tiny seed we find inside of an apple. Given the right environment and proper nourishment, that tiny seed can grow into a very large and productive fruit tree.

It's important that we surround ourselves with an environment and people that support us in being the person we want to be. We have only one person's life to live, and it's our own! We must live it according to our own dreams and visions; then we can share our good fortune with the world!

When the Student Is Ready, the Teacher Will Appear

Ready or not, the lessons keep coming at us. There's always something new to learn, and some of it falls into our laps, and we have to deal with it. There's a lesson in there somewhere!

When the student is ready, the teacher will appear, but the teacher may not be a person. It can be an experience or a situation we find ourselves in. We may get a fresh perspective on an earlier experience that we now see from a different point of view. Have you ever said to yourself, "That experience taught me a good lesson"? When the student is ready, the teacher will appear in one form or another.

The lessons are always there. We are the students who continue to grow and mature as we adjust ourselves to the ever-changing situations that we face. The lessons have been there all along, and they will continue to be there, just waiting for us to learn them. And when the student is ready, the teacher will appear.

There Ain't No Free Lunch

There's a price for everything. It isn't always financial, but there's always an exchange of one thing for another as we grow throughout our lifetimes. Perhaps we trade our time for money. Perhaps we give up going to one place in favor of another place of greater importance. Something must be given up for something else to happen. There is no vacuum in nature.

For artists to earn money with our talents, we may have to modify some of our personal forms of self-expression to create something that meets the client's tastes. It's not always an easy sacrifice for some of us, but as business-minded artists, we need to be willing to merge our thoughts with the needs of the client.

If we are currently experiencing life as a starving artist, perhaps we don't have to learn how to do better artwork; we probably just need to learn how to serve the needs of others. It's only in serving the needs of others that we get paid. The sooner we learn that lesson, the better things will be for everyone.

If we have an issue with the definition of commercial art, and we struggle with the idea of selling out our creative soul just to make a buck, consider the fact that if we are working at a job that does not require the use of any of our talents, we are already selling out our creative soul just to make a buck! We are completely ignoring the financial potential of our unique gifts. *Don't do that!*

Our talents can be our greatest assets if we develop them to the point where they have value to others. That's where the big bucks lie. We see the big bucks being paid to professional athletes and entertainers. The big money goes to those who develop their talents to the point where they serve the needs of the marketplace.

Our creative success is about using our unique gifts to serve people in ways that only we can do! With the right attitude, we can satisfy our creative spirit and fill our bank account at the same time.

How Do Dreams Come True?
By Believing in Them!

Dreams do come true, but first you have to have a dream! Most people don't. They have wishes, but wishes are not the same as dreams. By dreams, I don't just mean the kind of dreams we have when we are sleeping; I mean the kind of dreams that motivate us, the kind of dreams that inspire us to take action and do something.

Dreams are motivators. Dreams do not require us to work on them, because they have the power to work on us. Having a dream of something bigger than our present situation is a motivator. A dream is an intangible image or belief that takes root in our thinking and won't let us ignore it. Dreams inspire us and energize us, and they give us a reason to get up every morning.

A dream is a vision blended with the powerful emotion of desire. Wanting something is the starting point of having something. Without desire, there is no motivation to act. However, once we have enough desire for something, it becomes a clear image in our imaginations, and we begin to do things that are in harmony with that image.

Once we are clear about our dreams, our intellectual abilities will come up with ideas for solutions that can take us from wherever we are now to where we want to be. As we go through each day, our life will take on more of the activities that are associated with our imagined images, and in a very natural progression, our vision will manifest into a tangible product or experience.

That's how dreams come true!

For Dreamers and Believers and Wannabe Achievers

The path to get from where we are today to where we want to be, does exist. It's always been there, and it always will be. Perhaps it's been neglected or never recognized for what it is, but it does exist, and it's waiting to be discovered.

For people who believe there's more to life than what they have now, whether it's about wealth or health, better relationships or finding a deeper sense of purpose, the path to the perfect end result does exist if we can imagine it.

Quoting from the classic book *Think and Grow Rich* by Napoleon Hill, "What the mind of man can conceive and believe, it can achieve." For those of us who dream of doing something greater than we have accomplished so far, we must be believers too. We must believe in ourselves, and we must believe that we were meant to do, or have, something more than our current situation offers.

For those who want to achieve something significant, there's always a way to do it. We're all familiar with the phrase *when there's a will, there's a way*. We use our willpower to keep ourselves on track.

Once we've established our dreams in our imaginations, we must believe that it's possible to achieve them, even if other people don't understand or agree with us. That's when we must follow our hearts and cast our fate to the wind, so to speak. It's better to surrender to our dreams and see where they take us than it is to give in to our doubts and remain stuck with a lack of fulfillment.

Having a dream and committing to a goal is like giving ourselves a destination. It focusses our attention on why we do the things we do. Our life and our activities take on a new meaningfulness as they propel us toward the things we want.

The goal we pick is just a good reason to go on a journey. If it's really something we want, we will discover the steps or the path that will take us in that direction. If we seek, we will find, and if we knock, doors will open. But it's the journey and not just the destination that we want to experience. Life is just a series of experiences, tied together into what we refer to as a lifetime.

When we follow our heart, we make our lifetime a very interesting one!

The Money Comes, and the Money Goes, but the Lessons Are Ours to Keep

In the beginning of any career, it's not how much we earn but how much we learn that matters. The money comes, and the money goes with the everyday expenses of life, but the things we learn along the way stay with us for a lifetime.

Developing a solid foundation of business principles, along with our artistic skills, is a good recipe for success, since both elements are needed when it comes to earning money and feeling satisfied with our work.

Everything we do is built on a foundation of awareness, and we all start at our own beginning, then realize that there is no end! There's always more to learn and new ways to do things. As we grow, we enjoy taking on new challenges, and for the creative person, repetition is boring, and boredom is not an option!

Some things never change, and if we want our careers to endure, we need to anchor ourselves to those permanent foundations of successful living. A wise man builds his house on solid ground. Trends come and go. They pass through a society quickly, and they leave their mark, but trends never last.

Bloom where you're planted, and blossom when it's your season to do so. As Horace said in ancient times, "Carpe diem," or "Seize the moment!" Act now, in this moment, but if you want long-term success, build your career on principles of service and not just the trend of the moment.

The Creative Life Comes at a Price
You Have to Give Up Boredom!

For creative minds, boredom is not an option. It's usually not a problem either, because most creative people don't know what boredom is. In this day and age, there is so much new stuff showing up every day that experimenting with new techniques, new products. and different ways of doing things can be very inspiring for the creative mind. Follow where your curiosity leads you, but don't lose track of the business side of things if you want to make money.

It's rarely the experimenters who make the big bucks. They often spend their time dabbling around with things that interest them, but money is not their greatest interest. Curiosity and novelty drive the creative mind. That can be the greatest strength or the greatest weakness of the artist. We love to create things just to satisfy our curiosity. The creative process is its own reward. However, rather than the creator of the product, it's often the middleman who makes the big money by cashing in on the product's potential.

I love to experiment, and I do a lot of it, but when it comes to making money, I remind myself that I only get paid if I do something for others. I cannot be my own customer. It doesn't work that way.

The question becomes, "How can I serve the needs of others with my talent in a way that brings me pleasure?" That's a *big* question, but it needs to be answered. If we want to get paid, the things we produce must have value to someone before they will hand over their money. If we want to be happy, we must do things that keep us excited and enthusiastic about our work. When we find that balance of work and pleasure, life offers its rewards to everyone.

There Is No Competition
to Being Yourself

There is no competition to being yourself! Who else would you want to be, and who else would want to be you? We are each here for our own reasons. We each have our own gifts to give, and we have our own lessons to learn. If we use our gifts, we will learn our lessons, and life will be full of rewarding experiences. If we don't use our gifts, we will find ways to survive, but we will never experience the adventure or know the rewards of discovering our true nature.

When we are just starting our career, we may feel overwhelmed by other people's work. It may be intimidating, or it could be inspiring to us. The difference will be in our attitude. Each of us has our own gifts to offer, and to do that, we must learn our own lesson. No one is competing with us to do that. We have our own reasons for choosing the work we do, and no one is here to accomplish the exact same thing as someone else.

If five artists painted the same tree, each one would see the tree differently. While the subject would be the same, the end result would be unique from each artist. Everyone sees things from their own point of view. One artist might emphasize the colors, while another would focus on the shape. Another might be more interested in showing the environment the tree is in or a unique angle the tree is viewed from.

The point is that each of us has our own style because of the way we view the world, and one way is not better than another. There is no competition in how we look at things, so there is no competition in how we choose to express our point of view.

It's in the artist's emotional interests to express themselves in the most satisfying way, and it's in their financial interest to serve the needs of others. Success in the world of art lies in that middle ground where we satisfy our personal need to express ourselves by satisfying the creative needs of the marketplace.

If there is any competition, it comes from within, challenging ourselves to do a better job than we've ever done before.

Finding the Balance between Courage and Confidence

Courage is necessary when we do anything that scares us. Starting a new business, falling in love, and going away to school for the first time are all examples of common things we face at some point in our lives.

As artists, it takes courage to show our work to someone for the first time. It can be a frightening experience if we fear rejection or humiliation at the thought of failure. We all lack confidence when we try something new. That's where courage comes into play.

We must press on regardless! It's in our nature to do artwork, so we can't allow a little fear of rejection stop us from expressing our passion. The survival of our creative spirit depends on it. *Use it or lose it!*

Everyone starts at the beginning, wherever that may be for them. Then we expand by continually trying new things. With the curiosity to try new things, we come up with the courage to invest in something we want. We invest our time, some money, and perhaps most frightening of all, our hopes and our dreams of receiving a good return on our investment. With the things we learn from the experience, we gain the confidence to do it again.

With the determination to continue, we find the courage to take the next step, and with that, we develop the confidence that's needed to keep on keeping on.

The World Does Not Owe Us a Living

The world does not owe us a living, but we owe it to ourselves to be all that we can be. It's up to us to set the standards for our behavior and how we choose to use our time. It's our personal responsibility to go after the dreams and rewards we want to have in life, but the world does not owe those things to us.

It all starts with a desire for something, a vision or image in our minds of what the perfect end result would look like and what it would *feel* like when we live it every day. With our talents, we've been given a gift in its raw form, and we can shape that gift into something that other people would value and therefore be willing to pay for.

We only get paid in proportion to the value that other people place on our service, whether it's sweeping floors or shaping gold jewelry. Our present compensation is a measure of the value other people place on our time and service, or it's a reflection of what we are willing to settle for. The compensation we accept indicates the value we think our time and services are worth. A good question to ask ourselves is, what are we willing to settle for, compared to what are we committed to pursuing?

If we want to increase our wealth, we must find ways to increase the value of the work we do. That either requires serving more people or increasing our value to the current clients we serve. Of course, the best solution would be a combination of both.

The Eagle Flies above the Storm

An eagle is a bird of prey. It looks for opportunities and takes advantage of them when they arrive. Because of its sharp sense of vision and its keen hunting skills, when it sees what it needs, it goes for it! It often misses, but it is successful enough to keep itself alive.

When the winds pick up and a storm moves in, the eagle doesn't look for shelter; rather, it flies higher! It uses the wind to lift itself above the storm, where it can look down on the situation and wait for things to settle down once more.

As the winds of change stir up the dust around us, and we face the storms in our own lives, the secret is to raise our vision above the storm. We want to rise above it and see things from a higher perspective.

Change is constant, but storms don't last. There is no stability in a constantly changing environment, but with an understanding of the underlying principles of success, as leaders, we don't resist the change, but we embrace it, and we see it as an opportunity to move things forward in our ever-expanding world of higher consciousness.

PART 3

The Spiritual Side of Things

A Curious Mind Is a Curious Thing

Curiosity is the driving force behind all forward movement! We want to know more, and we want to understand things! We feel good when we figure things out, and our curiosity is rewarded. That's one of the things the human mind was made for, and it's a pleasure to use it!

We are the creative creatures on this planet. As humans, we have been given the power of thought, and we have a wonderful machine that we refer to as our body, which we can use to carry out our thoughts. As long as we are alive, we have the power and the ability to think and act. Action changes things, and when we act in accordance with our thoughts, we can affect the world around us.

Being alive and having a thought, along with having a mechanism to carry out those thoughts, gives us the power to create things and affect the world we live in. Another way of saying it is, the Spirit of Life that animates our minds and our bodies provides us with the power to live effective lives on this planet.

Mind, body, and spirit are the three elements that make all things possible. The mind creates the idea, the body performs the work, and the Spirit of Life provides the energy that the mind and body need to carry out the project.

With mind, body, and spirit, all things are possible.

The Teacher Points the Way, and the Student Points to the Teacher

There are always a few outstanding leaders in all walks of life. They demonstrate some form of greatness and set an example for others that proves what can be done in sports, business, entertainment, and other forms of leadership. Instead of learning from them, we often fall into the idolatry trap and think of them as being something special, even though most of them would be more than willing to tell you that they are no different in potential than you or I.

In religion, the Christians have Jesus, who points the way, and His followers who point to Jesus. "Jesus is the answer" becomes the mantra of the followers, but I think we miss the message by focusing on the messenger.

"I come as a pattern for mankind to follow. These things and greater can *you* do, for it is not I that doeth these things, but the Father within me. Know ye not that your body is the temple of the Lord and *His spirit dwells therein?*"

These words only become useful to us when we digest their meaning and apply them to our daily lives. When we no longer point to the teacher, but rather we become like the teacher, then we will have achieved what the teacher was pointing to all along.

What You See in the Mirror Is Not You

Have you ever looked in the mirror and said to yourself, "There's more to me than the mirror can see"?

I have my emotions, my thoughts, my memories. and my dreams, but none of that shows up in my reflection. The mirror only sees my body, but I am so much more than I can see with the eye. What I see in the mirror is not me. The real *me* lives within the body I see reflected in the mirror. But I am not my body! I am the life force that animates the body.

The real me is the part that's missing when they lay the body in the casket and say, "That's not him. That's just his body. He's gone on to a better place." If I'm the part that has gone on to a better place when my body lies in the casket, then I must be *that part now*; I just haven't separated myself from my physical body yet.

The real me is the power of life that animates the mind and body, and that power of life is eternal. The life that beats my heart and breathes my lungs is the same life force that was in my mother. Once her living egg was fertilized by the living seed of my father, she gave me a place within her body where I could grow my physical anatomy. Her life and my life were one and the same, until my body developed fully enough to leave the shelter of her womb and enter the outside world that I experience now.

The life force that was keeping my mother alive was the same power of life that was in my grandmother and my great-grandmother, each generation passing life on to the next generation through the process of the living male seed fertilizing the living female egg. The process is the same for all living things, plants and animals alike.

Life is eternal. It never ends. Life just keeps reproducing the next generation of things, as the Bible says in Genesis, "after their own kind." Today, we recognize that as genetics, but they didn't have that word when the book of Genesis was written.

The politicians have it wrong! Life *does not* begin at conception! Life is eternal! *Form* begins at conception, not life! The awareness of this fact can have a profound effect on our social attitudes, laws, and behaviors as society moves forward.

Regardless of our beliefs about the afterlife, we know there is more to us than our physical bodies, and we are so much more than the mirror can ever see!

The Perpetual Search for Balance

In the desire to live a full and creative life, we need to balance the four aspects of being human. The four elements to consider are our physical body, our emotions, our intellectual abilities, and our life energy. It's important to understand a little bit about each element so we can see how they interact with one another and how they show up in our everyday lives.

The physical body is the most obvious part of us. We know we have a body, and it gets much of our attention throughout our lifetime. We feed it, we groom it, and we nurture it with rest and exercise. If we take care of it, it tends to serve us well for several years.

Our emotions are our feelings. They drive many of our decisions, often unconsciously, and while they are invisible to the eye, they are very real, and they express themselves through our behavior. We all have the same menu of emotions to choose from, such as love, anger, fear, confidence, desire, joy, hatred, shame, and on and on. What makes us appear to be different from one another are the things that trigger our emotions and the particular emotions we choose to express at the moment.

The intellectual part sets goals and figures things out, makes plans for their achievement, and is data oriented. The intellect relies on reason and logic, rather than intuition and emotional values.

The fourth element of being human is the life force or the spiritual side of us. It's that energy that beats our hearts and breathes our lungs, so we don't have to consciously think about it. We simply refer to it as *being alive*. Without the life force, nothing else matters.

Most of us tend to rely on one element more than another, which creates an imbalance in our life. Perhaps we are more physically inclined than emotionally sensitive. Perhaps we rely on our intellectual skills more than our intuitive nature to guide us. The perpetual search for balance is our unconscious attempt to find an inner peace and confidence.

When these four elements are in balance, we have our physical health, we have the emotional ability to express ourselves in a positive way, we are intellectually smart enough to manage our time and earn the money we need, and we sense that we have a reason for being alive. Having a sense of purpose leads us to fulfilling our spiritual destiny.

Balance of the four elements is the key to personal power.

Living Life from the Inside Out

It all starts with imagination. If you can see it, you can be it, but you must believe that it's possible. Imagination + Belief = Having.

We've often heard the phrase "I'll believe it when I see it," but I think it's the other way around. It's only when we believe something that we are able to see it. How many times have you noticed something "for the first time," even though it's been that way all along? As our awareness shifts, the things we notice shift with it. Typically, we tend to focus our attention on the things we already believe to be true. We reinforce our sense of security that way.

"As you believe, so shall it be," at least for you. Every action we take in our life is based on our beliefs, even if our beliefs are mistaken. For example, if I see a flying insect and believe I might get stung by a bee, I'll swing my arms and move away, even if the flying insect was only a moth. We act according to what we *believe* to be true, not what necessarily is true.

Have you ever tried to change somebody's mind when they already believe something is a certain way? They will live their life according to their belief, because it is true for them, and even though I may have a completely different belief about the same subject, I will live my life according to my beliefs. Whatever results we create for ourselves, they will be in harmony with what we personally believe to be true.

Everything already exists, but we tend to ignore the things that don't fit into our familiar frame of reference. We only see the things we are in tune with. What we see in life reflects our level of awareness.

If we want things to be different from what we are currently experiencing, we must begin by imagining a different end result. We must have a vision of what that would look like, and we must *create the feeling* of what it would be like to have it. We can create the feeling that goes with it by believing that the desired result is possible. The more we feel it, the easier it is to believe it.

Our lives go in the direction of our beliefs, and our imaginations contain the images we associate with those beliefs. When we change those images, our lives change with them.

It all starts in our imagination, and the world we see around us reflects what we believe to be true within us. We experience our lives from the inside out.

Dreams Come True,
God Answers Prayers, and
Thinking Creates Our Experience

What do these things have in common? Other than the fact that they are true, they all involve the use of a mental image of some kind. When we have a big dream, we have an image in our minds of what that dream is about. When we pray, we have a vision in mind that we imagine as the desired result, and when we think, we think in pictures.

Pictures are the language of the mind. A picture is worth a thousand words, and learning to control the pictures in our mind gives us the ability to control the direction we take our lives in.

The mind is creative, and our mental pictures are the blueprints it uses to create our experiences. By first visualizing something in our imaginations, we become consciously aware of what we are looking for in the world around us.

Everything already exists in one form or another. We don't really create anything; we simply combine things in new ways to "create" new products. The exotic materials we use in today's technological world have been around for as long as the planet has, but we never had access to them, or we never combined the elements into the current combinations we're familiar with now.

By imagining something in our minds, we set the process in motion for it to manifest in our physical world. Have you noticed that when you decide to buy something specific, such as an automobile, you suddenly see that model of vehicle in many places? They didn't just suddenly show up. They've been there all along, but until our personal interest is engaged, we don't see what's there because we aren't focusing on it.

To cause a mental image to take shape in our physical experience, we must add the elements of emotion and belief. Desire for something is the starting point for having something. By believing that what we want is already a reality, that belief becomes the actualizing element that turns an image into a physical experience. If you don't believe it, you won't receive it, even if it lands in your lap.

Affirmations, Meditation, Motivation, and Inspiration

The use of affirmations and the practice of meditation are powerful tools in creating a successful life. Affirmations are statements we make to ourselves, consciously or unconsciously, that affirm a belief we hold to be true. We can make a conscious choice to affirm something good for ourselves, and we can repeat that affirmation over and over until it takes hold in our subconscious mind as a truth that we accept. Since we always act in harmony with our beliefs, the affirmations we accept to be true shape our current and future situations.

As adults, we can choose to work with our conscious affirmations. The challenge is to overcome the unconscious affirmations we learned throughout our childhood. Those beliefs were picked up without much choice on our part. We accepted the only version of reality that we were given. As adults, we can begin to reaffirm a new version of reality, based on a different understanding of the past, or simply because we want to imagine a different future. If we have free will, it shows up in the freedom to choose what we want to imagine and what we choose to believe to be true.

Meditation is the act of closing our eyes and remaining aware of the images or thoughts that come to mind. By paying attention to our self-talk and by being aware of our own words and the images that play over and over in our imagination, we become aware of the things that are affecting our attitudes and the way we view the world.

That stuff you see and hear is *you talking to you*! Listen to what you are telling yourself!

Those words and images are *your* version of reality. If they're working for you, keep them, but if you want something to change in your personal life, start by changing what you see and say in your inner life.

Meditation is a way to embrace the inner life, or the imagination, as the central command center for all of our attitudes and activities.

Motivation is that driving force to achieve something. Motivation is based on a desire for something not yet accomplished. Motivation is energy wanting to be put to good use.

Inspiration comes from somewhere within us, and it works *through* us. Inspiration takes motivation to another level as it causes us to look deeper within ourselves and we discover and work with our creative source. When we are inspired, we reach higher levels of accomplishment by reaching a deeper understanding of the true nature of our human existence.

The Imagination, the Physical Body, and Life Itself

With the three elements of imagination, the physical body, and the energy of life, we are complete human beings. When we use our imaginations, we make use of our mind. Our body moves in harmony with the thoughts and decisions we make with our mind, and those thoughts and actions can only happen when we are alive and have that spiritual force we call "life" expressing through us. Take away that life element, and our mind stops communicating, and our body dissolves rather quickly.

No one can deny that life is real, but no one can describe what *life* looks like or where it's located. Life is that invisible force that keeps our hearts beating and our lungs breathing. While we often label our personal activities as being *our life*, the power of being alive is "life" itself, expressing through our minds and bodies.

The Bible says that God created man in His own image. It is a simple concept, and we've heard it all before—mind, body, and spirit, the three parts of the Holy Trinity, often referred to as the Father, Son, and Holy Ghost. They are the same three parts of being human. We have a mind, we have a body, and both are powered by the spiritual force we call "Life".

Life is not a physical thing. It can't be seen or located in any particular place. It's in me, and it's in you, and it's in everything that is alive. We have our individual thoughts, and we have our individual bodies, but the invisible power of life is shared by all living things, plants and animals alike.

Welcome to the Age of Aquarius

I never paid much attention to astrology, and I certainly didn't take the daily newspaper's horoscope with any seriousness. However, considering the rapid changes going on around me, I sense a deeper reality at work, and I've taken a deeper look at things.

Just for a little background on where I'm coming from, I went to a Lutheran grade school for the first eight years of my education. I learned my Bible stories, and I memorized my passages, and they have served me well throughout my lifetime.

My father was Catholic, and my mother was Lutheran, so I always felt that different religions were okay. I knew nothing about Muslims, Jews, Hindus, or Buddhists, but in my small world, religions didn't matter. Today, as I see how different religious perspectives affect a wide variety of social behaviors, I find the different philosophies to be interesting, and they play a bigger role in my view of why the world is the way it is today.

Let's start this discussion about the age of Aquarius, back about six thousand years ago. Astrologically speaking, back then we were in the age of Taurus the Bull. I'm not a historian, but this was about the time when humanity was learning to domesticate cattle. During this time, a man's wealth was measured in cattle, and it was a common practice for the father of the bride to give a dowry of cattle to the newlyweds when they got married.

An astrological period of the zodiac lasts about two thousand years, and following the era of Taurus the Bull, the zodiac entered the age of Aries the Ram, or the Arian age. This would have been about four thousand years ago, or approximately two thousand years before the birth of Jesus. Biblically speaking, this would be about the time of Abraham, as told in the twenty-second chapter of Genesis. In this Bible story, Abraham is told to build an alter and sacrifice his son as a way of proving his love for God more than anything on earth.

When it was time to make the sacrifice, Abraham sees a ram caught in a thicket, and he sacrifices that instead. This can be seen symbolically as the beginning of the Arian age. The social laws during this time were largely based on the attitude of an eye for an eye and a tooth for a tooth. Struggle and violence were a common way of life for much of the evolving world.

The Arian age lasted about two thousand years, and according to astrology, we then entered the Piscean age. Pisces is a water sign, and the fish is its symbol in the zodiac. Jesus comes along about this time, and He does all sorts of things related to water. He walks on water, changes water into wine, baptizes His followers with water, calms the storm, and so forth.

He basically announces that the law of the new age is no longer an eye for an eye and a tooth for a tooth, but "I say unto you, forgive your brother seventy times seven." Forgiveness becomes a central topic of His teachings, and for this, they nail Him to the cross, and He says, "Forgive them for they know not what they do."

His death becomes a defining moment in the Christian movement, and it can be seen symbolically as the beginning of the Piscean age. The fish becomes the symbol of the Christians, and it is still being used today. The Catholics eat fish on Fridays, and the pope's headdress (called a miter) is shaped like the open mouth of a fish. These are all Piscean symbols and images.

Back in the age of Taurus the Bull, humanity went through the stage of domesticating cattle and learning to do all the things that were needed to provide for them. During the Arian age, civilizations fought and conquered and redefined each other. During the Piscean age, humanity learned a lot about water and what it can be used for.

In the early stage of the Piscean age, all boats were made of wood, for the obvious reason that wood floats. By the end of the Piscean age, all large ships were made of materials that do not float on their own, because the minds of men had expanded to realize that it is the shape that makes things float, rather than the materials. That awareness signified a profound evolution of human consciousness!

During the Piscean age, we also learned how to use water to generate electricity with hydroelectric dams, and how to use water as steam to power machines and heat buildings. The Piscean age was the age of water, but we're no longer in the Piscean age.

Today we are in the age of Aquarius. Aquarius is an air sign. Just as the age of Taurus the Bull brought strides of growth in domesticating cattle and the growing of crops to support it, the age of Aries the Ram led to shaping humanity into societies, and the Piscean age brought great strides in water development. Now the Aquarian age is promising to bring great strides in our consciousness of air and space.

I figure we entered the Aquarian age about the time the Wright brothers flew their first flight. Think about it. For as long as humanity has been on the face of this earth, we have wanted to fly but only dreamed about it. For millions of years, we thought about things that flew, but we never got off the ground.

It wasn't until all the necessary elements were in place, such as the mechanical engine, the shape of the wing, the balance of weight to power, and so forth, that humankind's consciousness reached the level of understanding that was needed to get off the ground. That represented another profound change in humankind's mental evolution.

Once one or two people had figured out how to get off the ground, it didn't take long for many more people to copy the idea and get into the business of perfecting the new machine. Along came World War I, and the use of the airplane was seen as a benefit we had to have. With the life-and-death conditions of war, the airplane took major leaps in development in a very short period of time! Urgency! Life and death! The pressures of war often force us to discover, improve, and perfect certain technologies. We see that repeated again and again throughout history.

After the war, the airplane became civilized to a degree, and society was given the benefit of airmail. A short time later, we entered World War II. During this period, our understanding of air and space expanded rapidly once again. We developed radar and the technologies of improved communications. The propeller-driven airplane quickly evolved into jets, and after the war, society was given the commercial airline industry we have today. From jets, the military quickly developed rockets, and we entered the space age. We started putting satellites into orbits, and we put a man on the moon.

As we entered the age of Aquarius (an air sign), humankind's consciousness expanded to the point of understanding the principles that were needed to fly. We entered the age of flight, then quickly moved into the jet age, then the space age, and today we live in the age of the internet, which was originally designed for the military but now has been turned over to the general public for use in private enterprise.

When it's time for humanity to change, some catastrophic event seems to force us to progress rapidly. World War I forced the rapid development of the airplane. World War II pushed the technology into the jet age. Fear of our enemies pushed us into the space age with satellites that gave us the age of the internet. The worldwide COVID crisis forced the digital technology companies to expand their services quickly to meet the sudden need of the home-based workers. A crisis is a motivator for expanding technologies.

Today, we do almost everything through the air. Our cell phones have no wires attached, but I can get my news and entertainment on my hand-held device. I can send pictures and transfer money around the world in seconds, without having to leave my house. I can be in another part of the world and still keep watch on my house with a home security app.

We've learned how to fly drones around the globe from a central command post far away, and our automobiles are able to take us places without a driver. Visionaries for our future see space travel as a form of entertainment, where we can travel to a space resort in a similar way that we book a cruise on a ship today.

Welcome to the age of Aquarius. This is only the beginning!

Printed in the United States
by Baker & Taylor Publisher Services